Name

Start Date

End Date

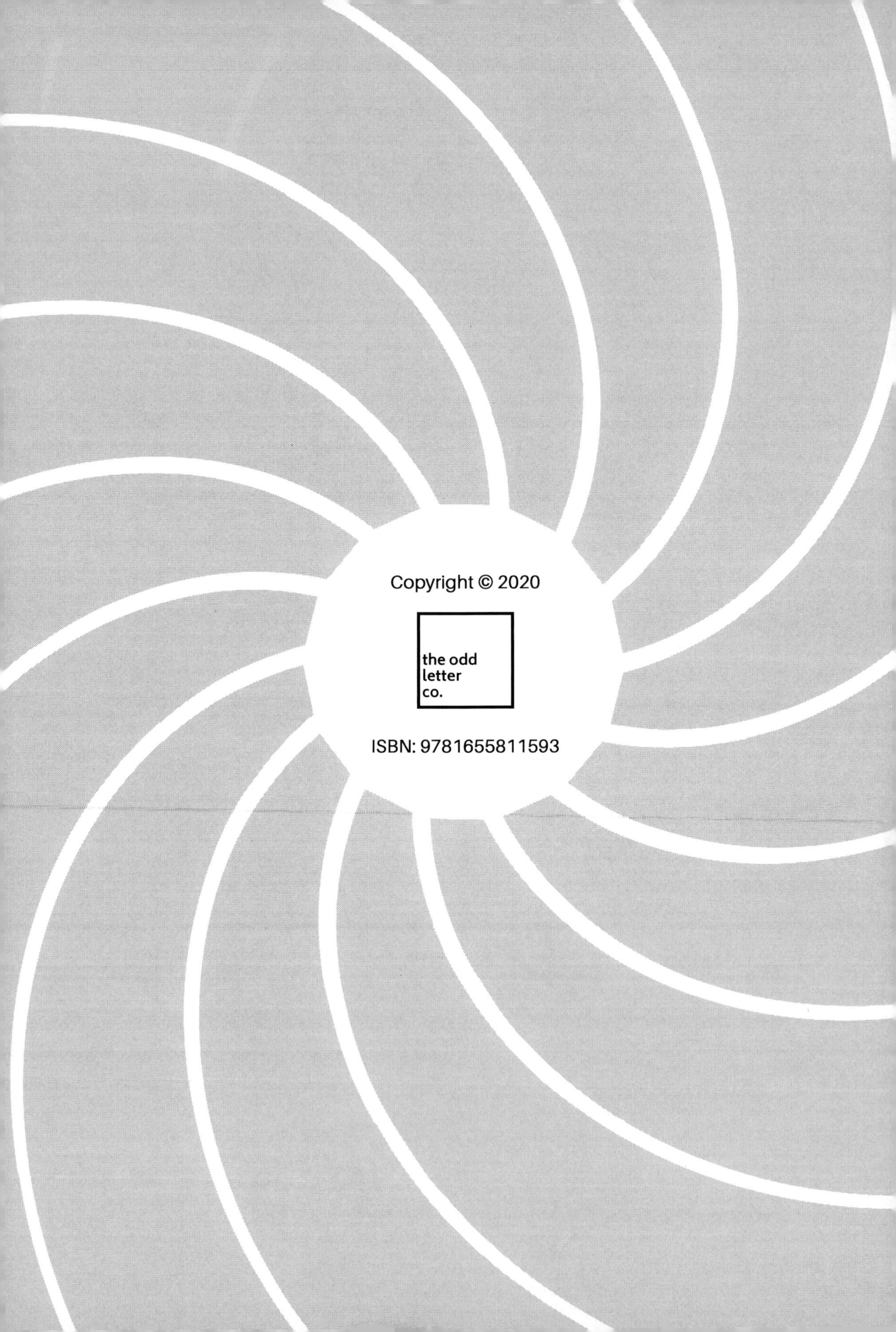

ISBN: 9781655811593

Your Assignments

This 30-day assignment challenge is designed to motivate you to grab the camera or smartphone and to start taking pictures more consciously. You can learn new aspects and dimensions of photography or features of your (new) camera, or simply put your passion for photography into action.

You will be given a topic to capture. The choice of camera, lens, settings, etc., will be up to you. Let your creativity run free, only then can you discover your potential. When you are satisfied with your result, paste the picture into this book to successfully complete the assignment of the day.

Included are tips and brief explanations for each challenge. Of course they are only short hints, because long explanations would slow your shutter speed and lose your focus. :)

Have fun and enjoy your assignments!

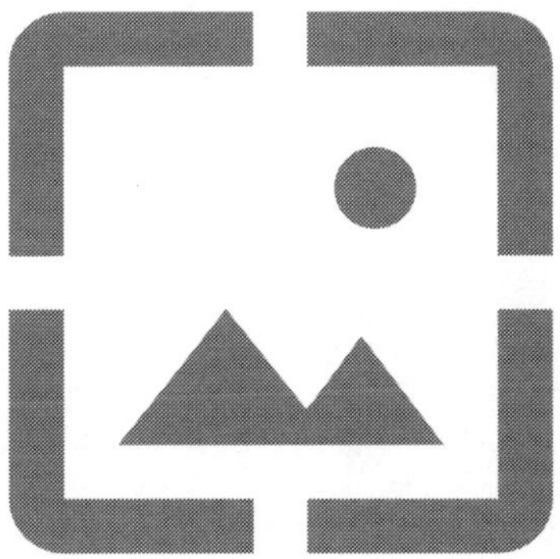

Symbols

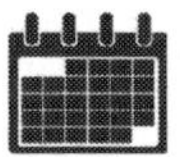

Date

Weather conditions

Time

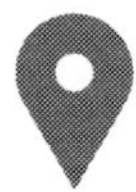

Location

Camera

Notes, ideas, problems, solutions, details about editing, results, ...

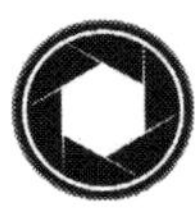

Lens

Lighting

Other equipment like a portable folding reflector, etc...

Check the box if you use flash

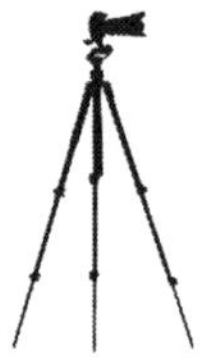

Check the box if you use a tripod

Write down settings like shutter speed, white balance, ISO, aperture, etc...

MY CAMERA EQUIPMENT

Day 1

FAMILY

Nobody should look stiff and cramped. The models should assume a relaxed, natural pose, with perhaps their weight shifted to one leg or a hand in pocket. The most important requirement here is to add a level of depth to the story of this family picture.

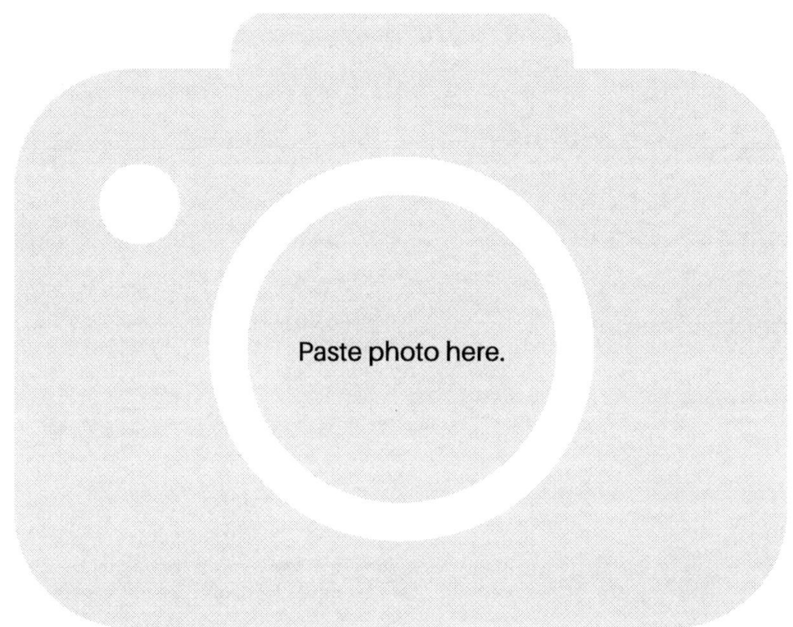
Paste photo here.

☆☆☆☆☆

Day 2

CLOUDS

Bad weather is a landscape photographers friend. Clouds can be so beautiful when illuminated by the sun or rolling along a windswept sky. They can look surreal with high contrast and visible structure. Use a polarizing filter, if you have one, when encountering all the different forms and varieties of clouds.

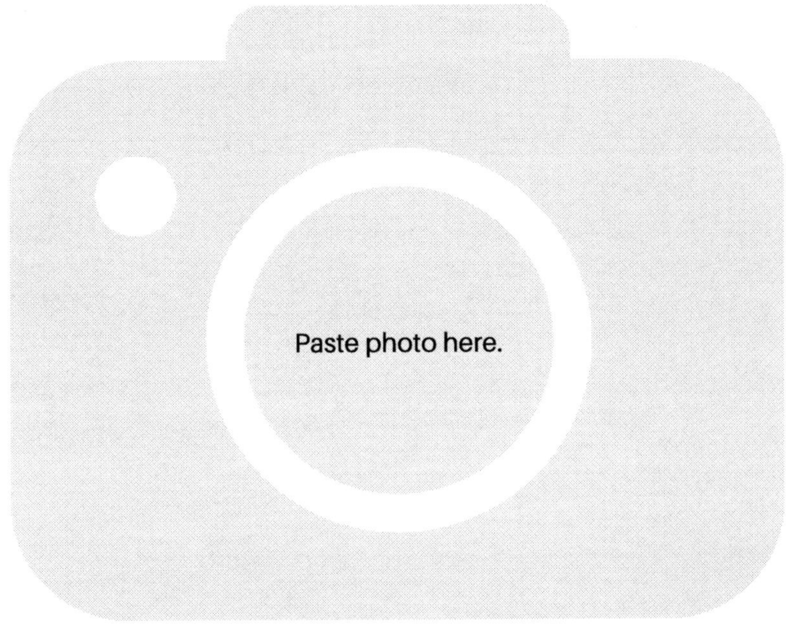
Paste photo here.

Day 3

LOVE

That wonderful feeling towards someone or something that induces a strong sense of affection. Capture love the way you understand it to be, whatever form that may take.

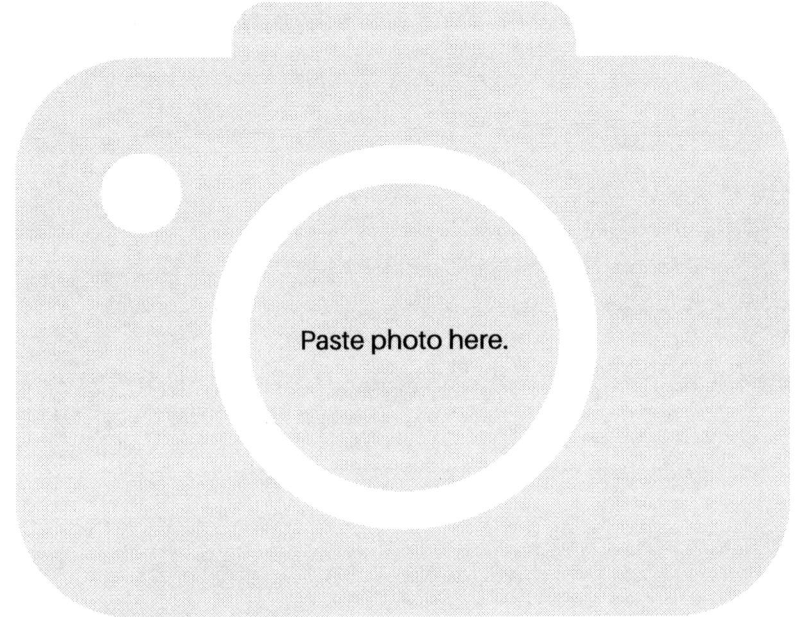
Paste photo here.

Day 4

BLACK AND WHITE

The perfect time to break some rules of color photography; now you can take a picture in bright sunlight, for example, where there are strong contrasts. When shooting in black and white it helps to think in terms of black and white, then you focus on less, because in black and white photography, less is more.

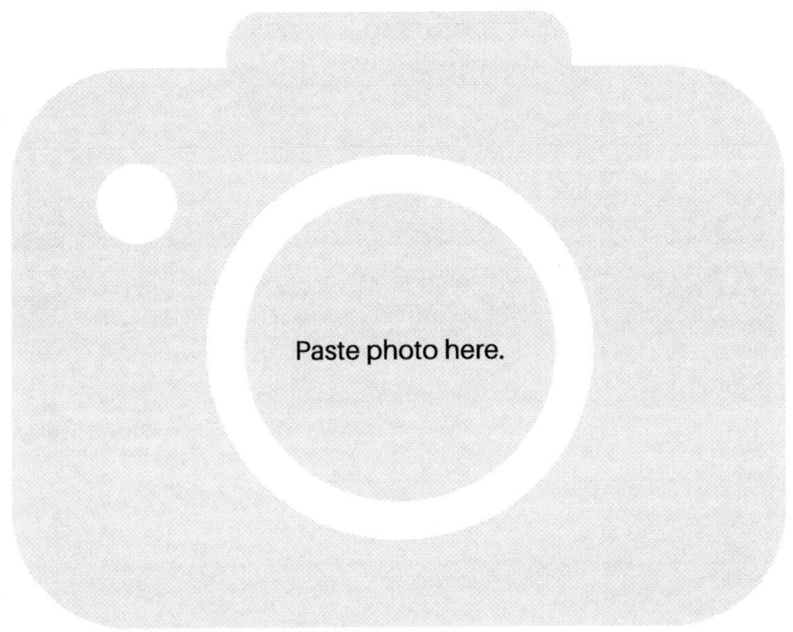
Paste photo here.

Day 5

CHILDREN

Shooting them from above makes children seem smaller than they already are. Taking pictures at eye level changes the story you tell. Most children move quickly and unpredictably. Spontaneous photos and shots in burst mode make sure that you capture that special moment.

Paste photo here.

☆☆☆☆☆

Day 6

GREEN

No, not green screen. Green leaves, meadows or any other green object that would make a nice photograph.

Paste photo here.

☆☆☆☆☆

Day 7

TEXTURE & PATTERNS

Patterns and textures can be found everywhere, not only in nature, such as on wood or ice crystals, but also on house facades, fabric or sidewalks. Seek and you shall find.

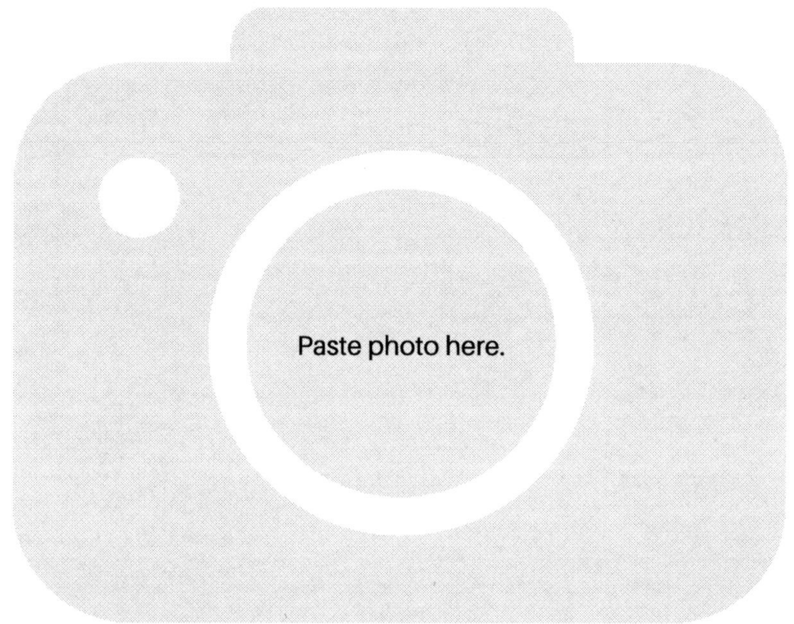
Paste photo here.

Day 8

BABIES

Here you can take a closer shot if, for example, hands or feet are photographed. It is best to have other objects in the picture, such as the hand of an adult, to show the proportions of how small they are.

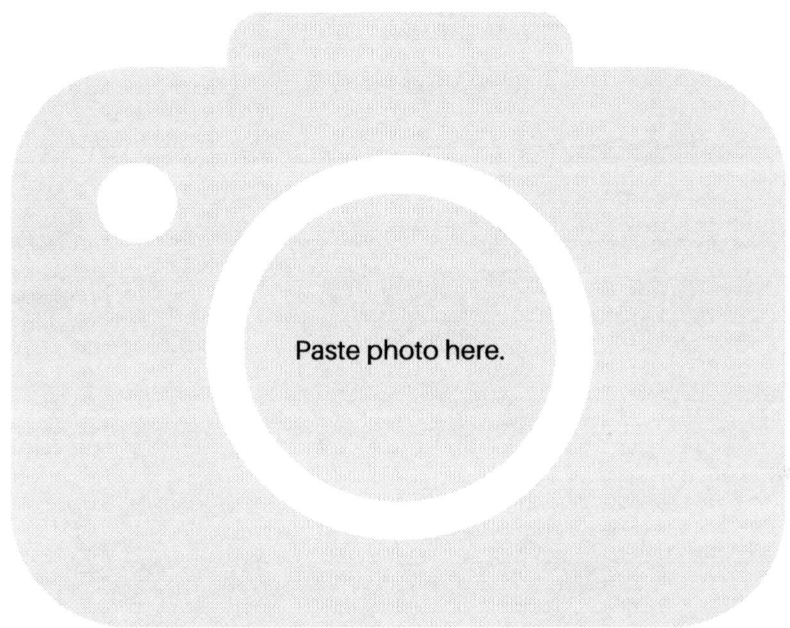
Paste photo here.

☆☆☆☆☆

Day 9

LANDSCAPE

Not only the landscape itself, but using objects in the foreground or background, such as plants, trees or mountains, can make a landscape photo special. Also popular are reflections in lakes or making milky looking streams — long exposures — using the shutter speed feature of your camera.

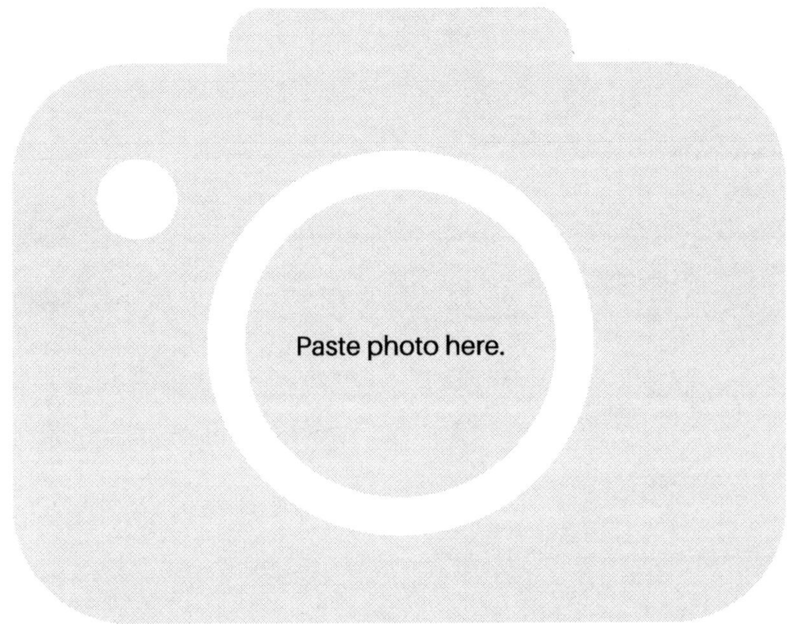
Paste photo here.

Day 10

NIGHT PHOTOGRAPHY

Especially in night photography we come to realize again: Photography is all about light and shadow. Whether it's city lights or stars, in the dark you almost always find a light source to play with.

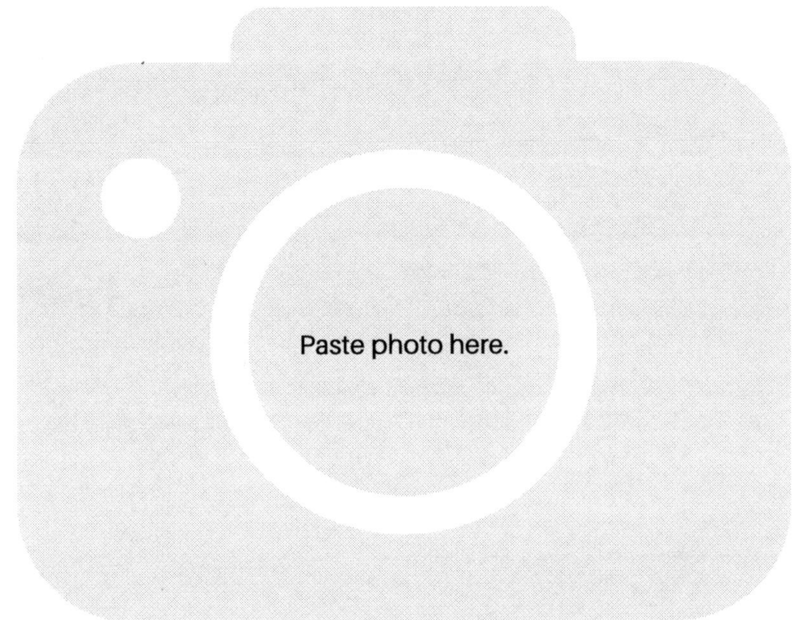
Paste photo here.

Day 11

YELLOW

Flowers, sunbeams, pineapples, or front doors in London - this week we are looking for something yellow. The challenge here is: can you put the yellow even more in the spotlight? Can you emphasize the yellow but still keep it stylish?

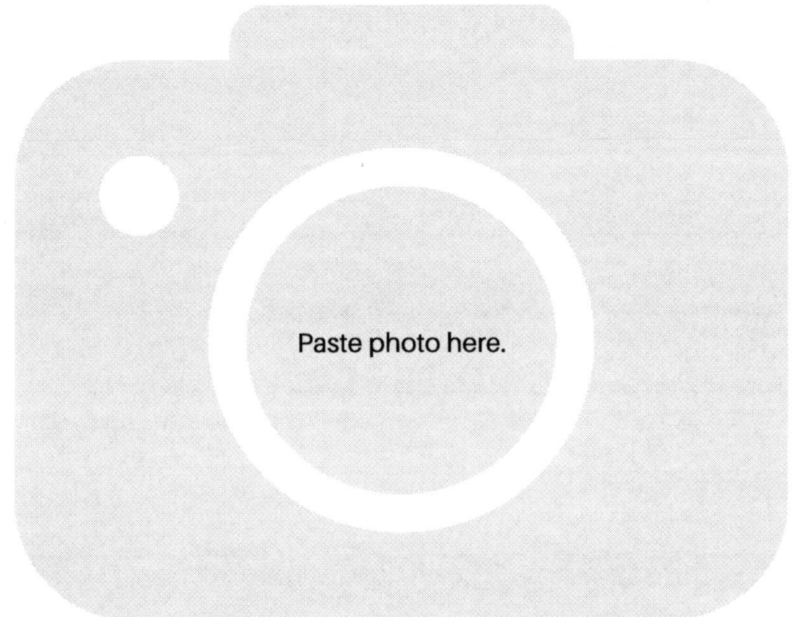
Paste photo here.

Day 12

SENIORS

Paying attention to seniors makes them happy and brings a very special smile to their faces. Especially when they are asked to serve as models. Capture the wisdom and the beauty when teeth and laugh lines appear, and silver hair shimmers... #HappyOldPeople

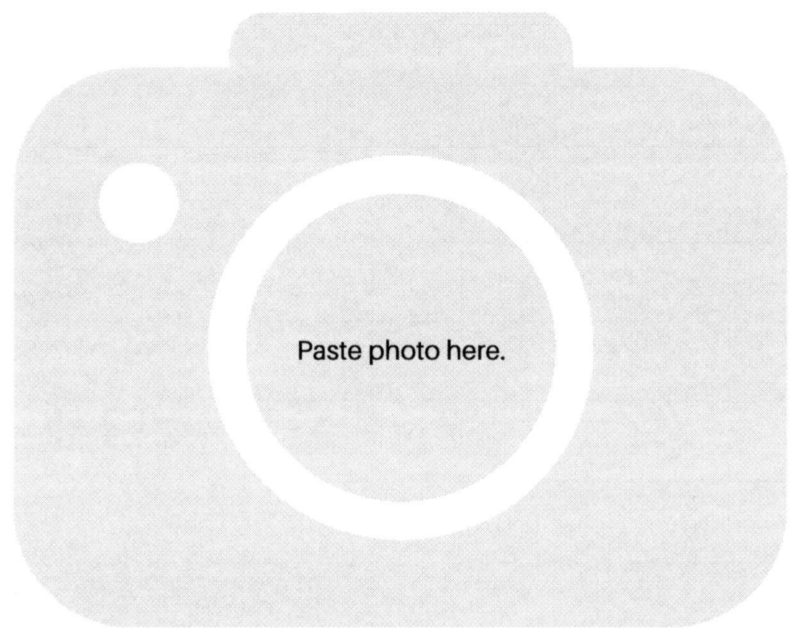
Paste photo here.

☆☆☆☆☆

Day 13

SELF-PORTRAIT

A self-portrait teaches you what it's like to be a model in front of the camera. It's easier to put yourself in the positions you want. Photographing yourself also means getting to know yourself, becoming aware of your inner feelings and the person you really are.

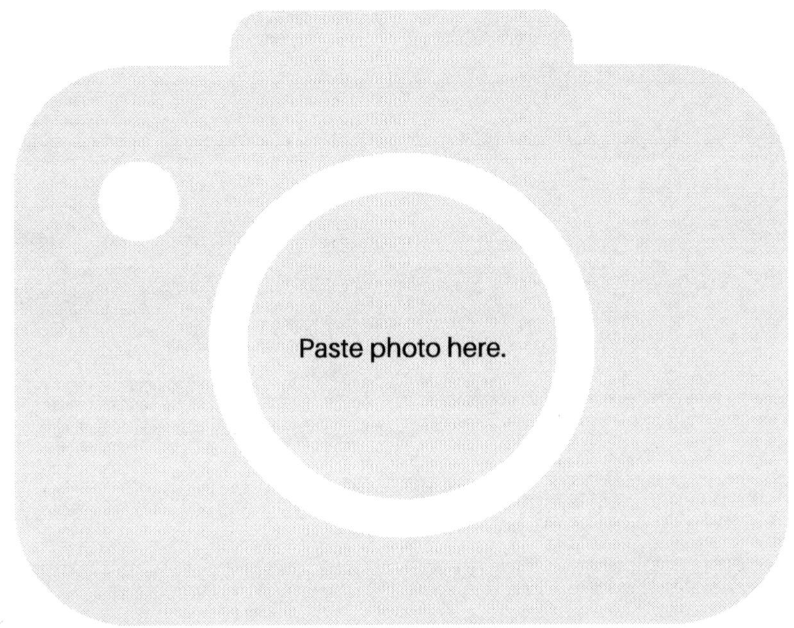
Paste photo here.

Day 14

FOOD PHOTOGRAPHY

When it comes to food, it is important to observe the rule of odds. If you have only 2 muffins in the picture, the viewer's gaze jumps from one muffin to the other. If there are 3, 5 or 7 muffins, the photo looks more harmonious. Interesting backgrounds such as a table made of wood or marble also accentuate the food.

Paste photo here.

Day 15

WATER

A brook. A lake. The river. The sea. Waterfalls and fountains. Take your pick. Children splashing around, a single drop or a vast expanse of water. There is a lot of room to explore your creativity, it's all up to you.

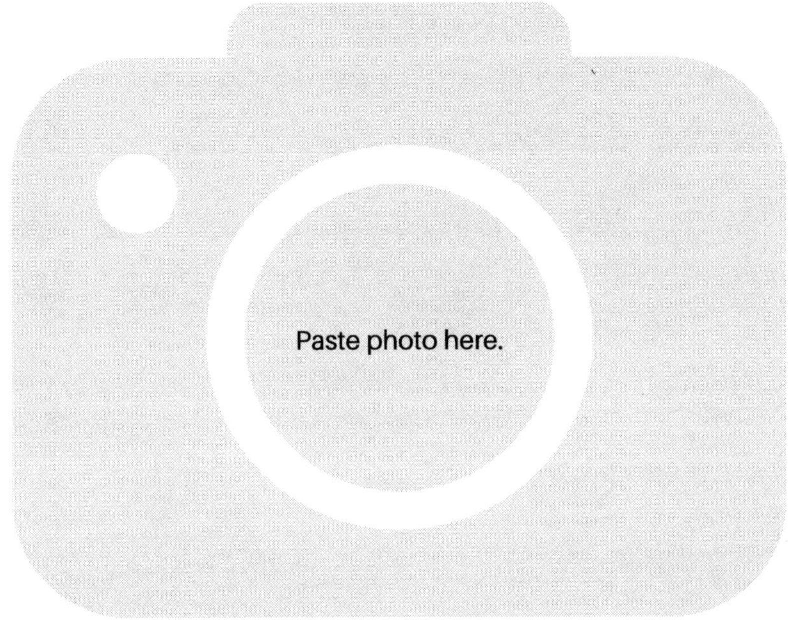
Paste photo here.

Day 16

STREET PHOTOGRAPHY

A street photo isn't necessarily full of people, but when there are people they don't always have to be photographed from the front. Capturing street life means unarranged, spontaneous crossover. There's always something going on and the key is to grab the essence of the moment.

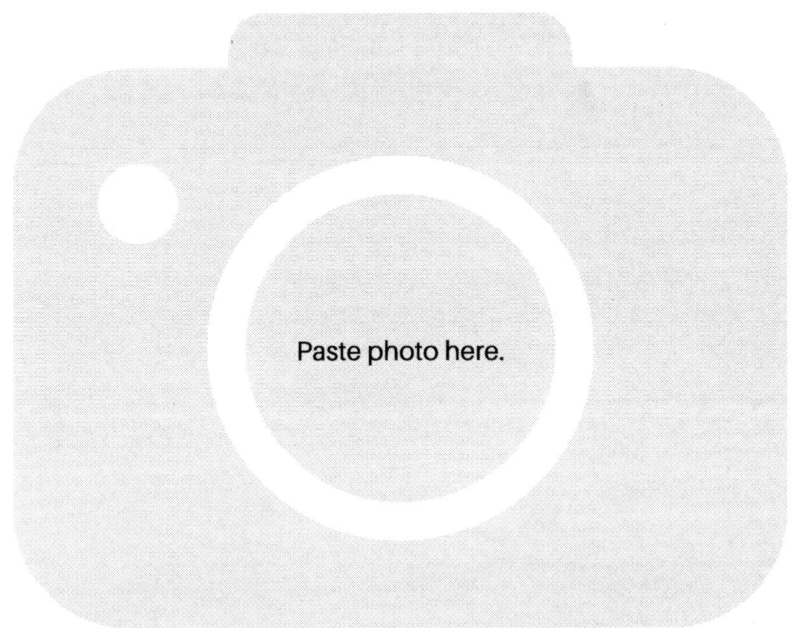
Paste photo here.

Day 17

ARCHITECTURE

Skyscapers, castles, bridges, abandoned buildings, derelict cottages, new buildings, garden sheds and everything else that has been created by human hands are in the spotlight this week. Use all that you've learned of composition and aesthetics to get the best possible shot.

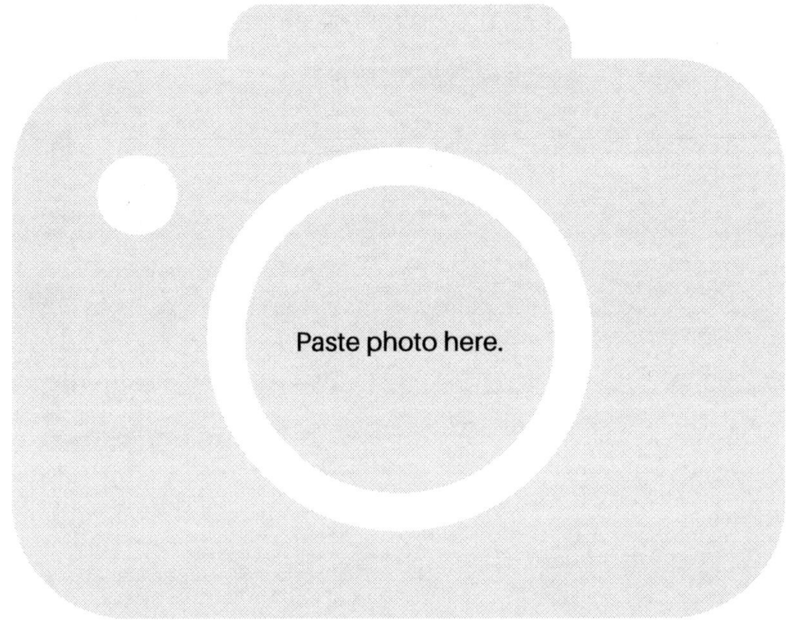
Paste photo here.

Day 18

COUPLES

They could be gazing into each other's eyes or staring out of frame. Sitting, standing or dancing - the possibilities are endless to photograph a couple. No suitable couple found among friends and family for this challenge of the week? Maybe it's worth taking a look in the animal world. Swans, ducks or horses often travel in pairs.

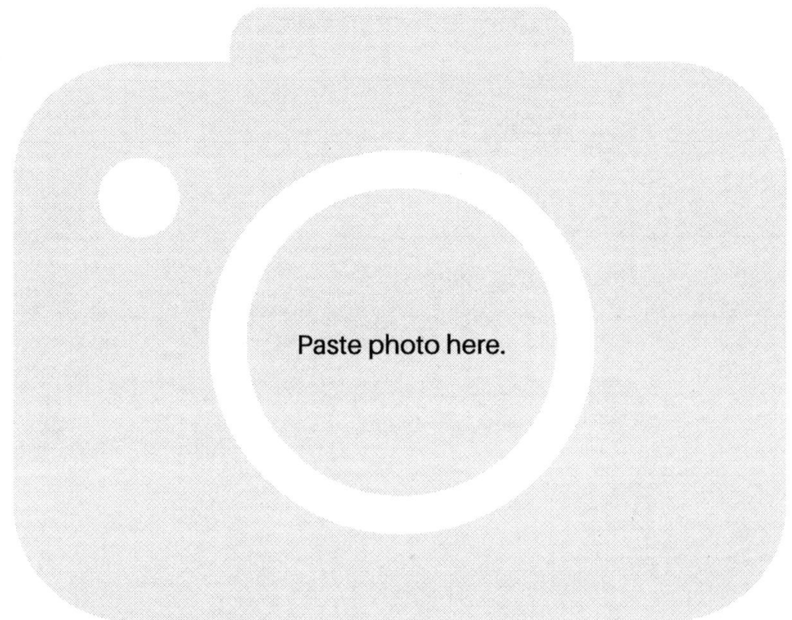
Paste photo here.

Day 19

FLASH

It is avoided by some photographers with the assertion that it is "fake" - the flash. But light is light, whether artificial or natural. What matters most is how you use the light and what you create from it. This week the flash should be used consciously. It's there for a reason, find out why, then master it.

Paste photo here.

☆☆☆☆☆

Day 20

SILHOUETTE

They seem mysterious because they hide everything but the outline. All you need is a bright background in which the object receives little or no light. If the sun is quite low and the object is illuminated from behind, this is a good time to press the shutter button.

Paste photo here.

Day 21

TREES

Trees are generally easy to find, sometimes right in front of your doorstep. A photo of a lush canopy or gnarled roots, a tree in full bloom or bare in winter, create a unique subject that really gets across what you want to express.

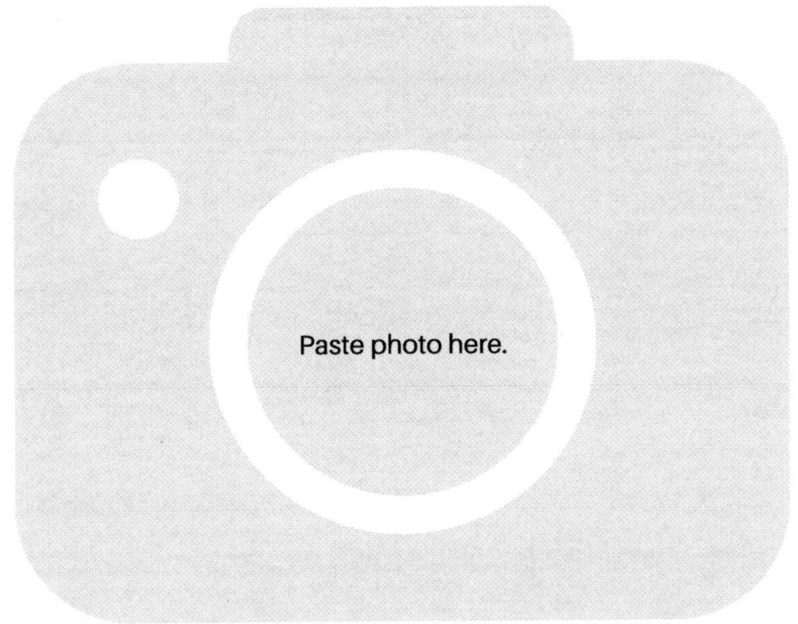
Paste photo here.

Day 22

HANDS

One on top of another, folded, formed into a heart, holding something, showing something, wearing a ring, tattooed, open, clenched or simply around the hip. With our hands we can express just about anything, it's no wonder we have sign language. What will you express with your photograph?

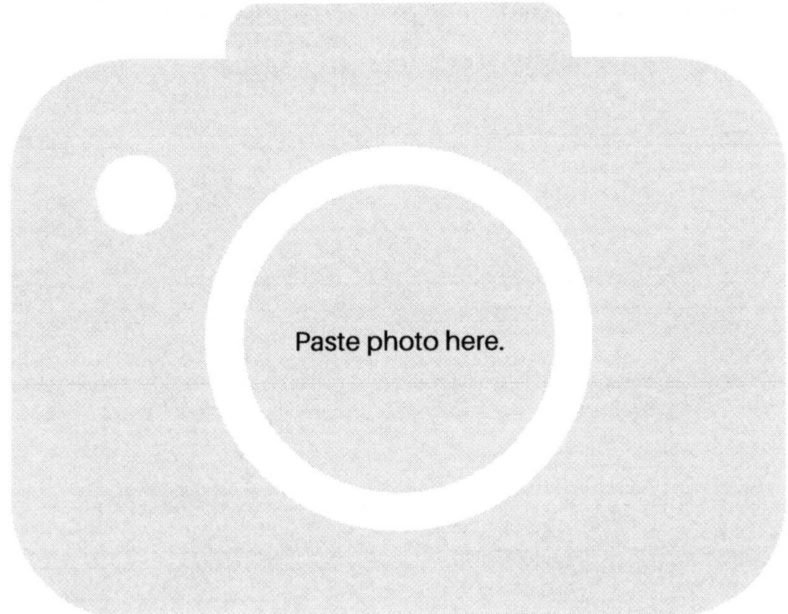
Paste photo here.

☆☆☆☆☆

Day 23

ANIMALS

From wildlife to house pets, patience is required when photographing animals. Know your subject well, including behavior and characteristics before you start photographing. The animal and environment are paramount. Your photography should be like a spectre in their background. No disturbing and no destruction. Once this is established, take amazing photographs!

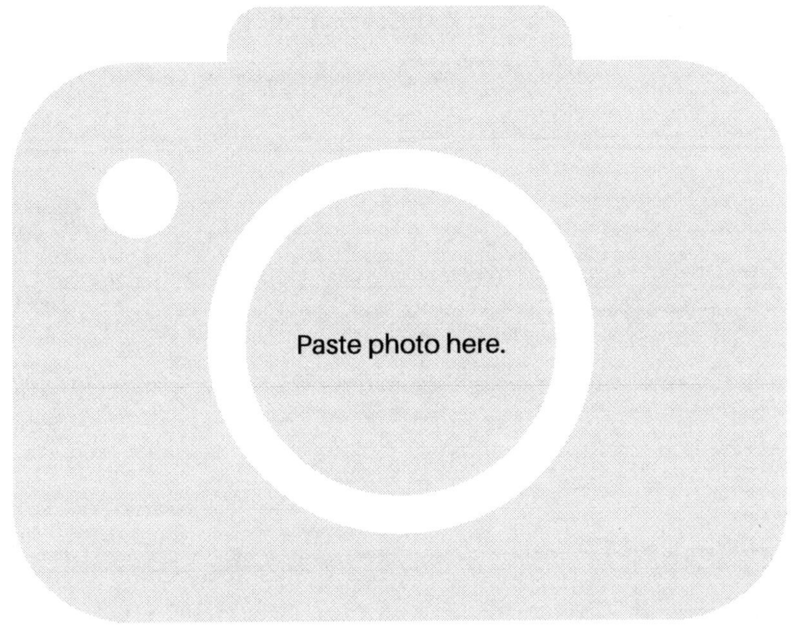
Paste photo here.

Day 24

WIND

The effects of wind can be seen in obvious places. A smoke stack, wind turbine, and trees. There are more subtle and rare ways to catch its effects, too. A person carrying an umbrella, swirls in the clouds, a bird struggling in flight, kites and long hair in a swept up mess. Whatever you do, be safe.

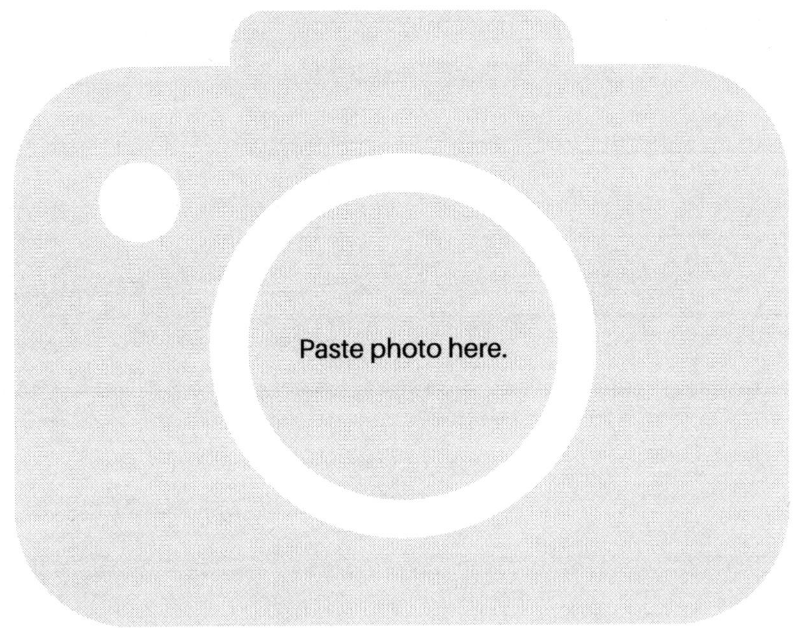
Paste photo here.

Day 25

YOUR STYLE

Every photographer has his or her own individual style, something they are really good at. After 42 weeks of this photography challenge, what are you particularly good at or find more than interesting? What is your specialty? Let the answer to this be your guide in finding your own personal style. Build on it and let your light shine.

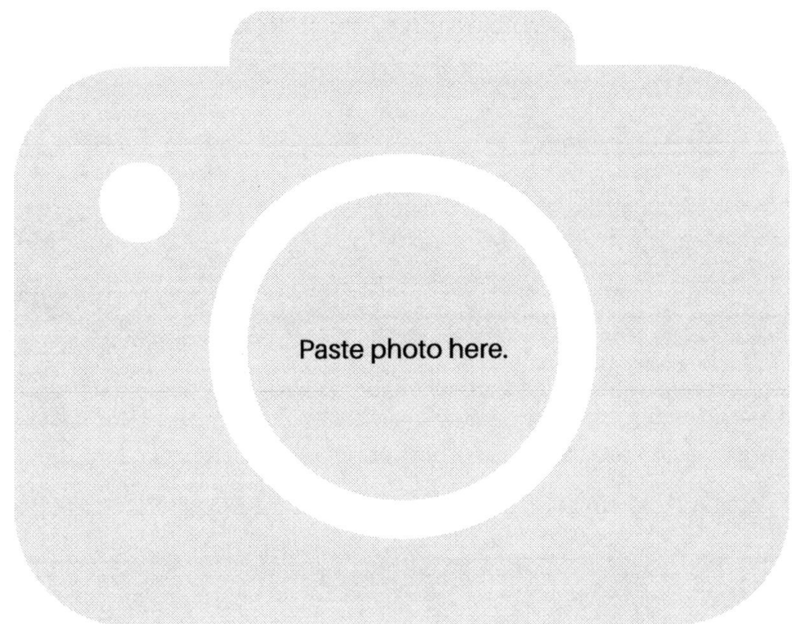
Paste photo here.

☆☆☆☆☆

Day 26

SPOOKY

The cellar stairs, gothic castles or abandoned buildings, almost anything plus darkness - horror is an art unto itself. At first glance you get goose bumps without hearing or feeling anything. An appeal to the vulnerable aspects of vision without being exploitive, sight is perfectly sufficient.

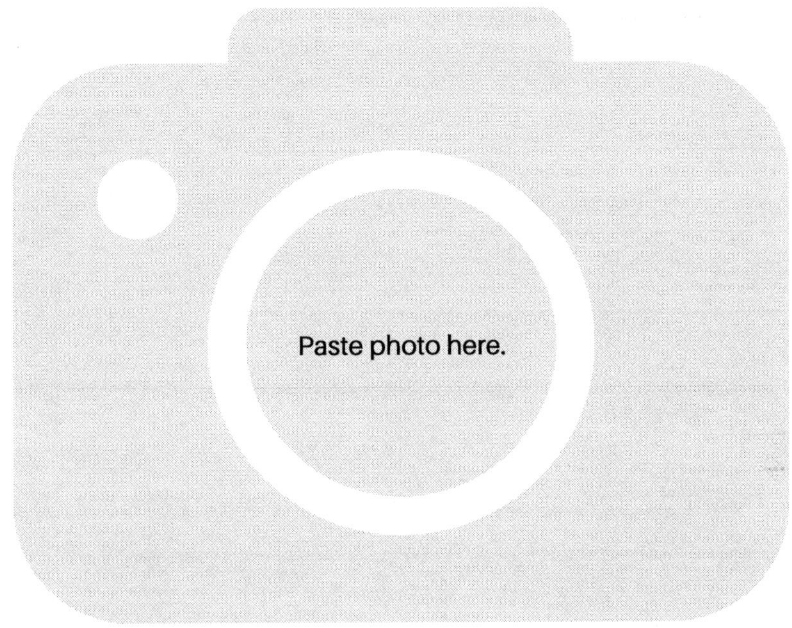
Paste photo here.

Day 27

PHONE PHOTOGRAPHY

Never underestimate the capabilities of a cell phone camera, the technology has come a long way. Time to learn a phone's features and how to use them. If you have been always photographing with a phone up to now, then try new settings this time, ones you've never used before. Let's see what comes of it.

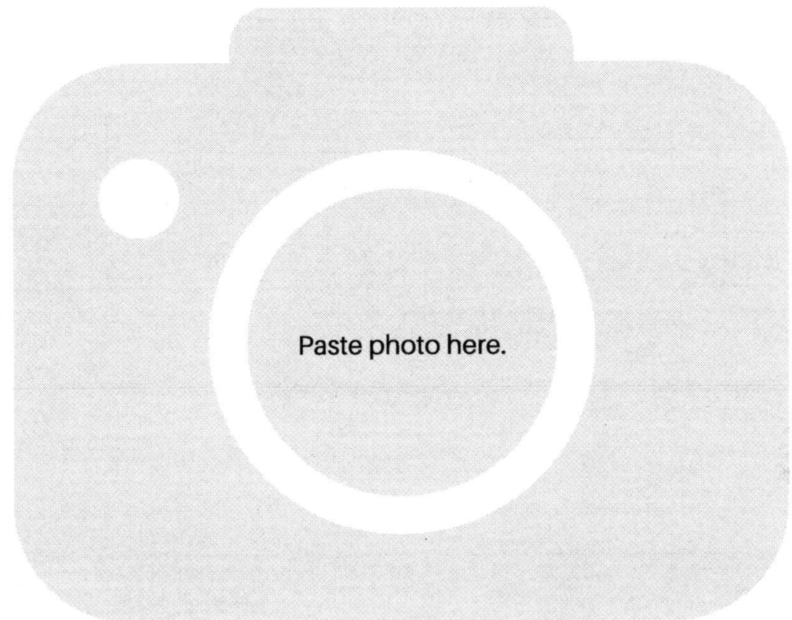
Paste photo here.

Day 28

BEVERAGES

A freshly poured cola, sparkling water, clamato juice with salt on the rim, foam on a latte, cream clouds in coffee, smoothies - from the making, presenting, even spilling of the drink - all this offers itself to be photographed. Use a spray bottle to mist the glass of a cold drink. Back or side lighting for transparent beverages.

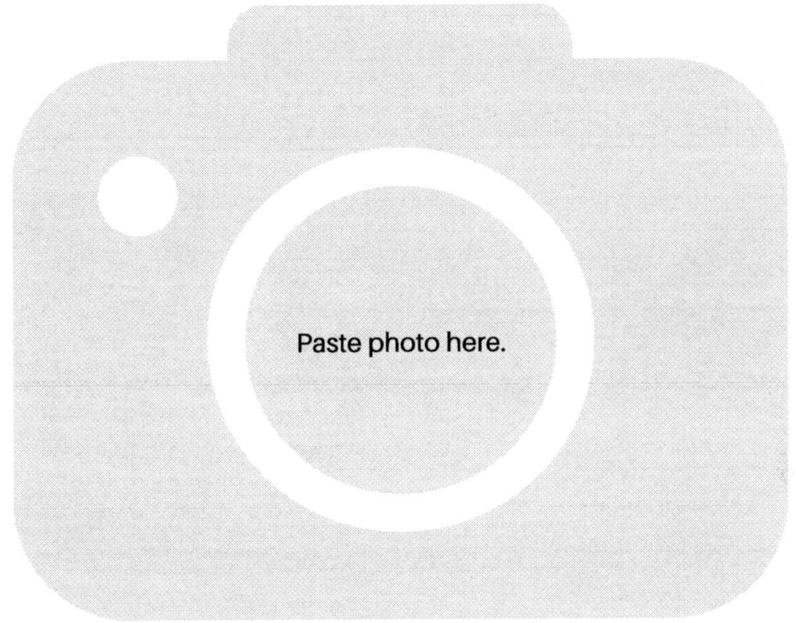
Paste photo here.

Day 29

CLOTHING

A laundry basket, worn shoes, a hole in the socks, a special dress, hanging, lying, wrinkled - we wear them every day, so this week we can pay a little more attention to them and make a nice subject out of it.

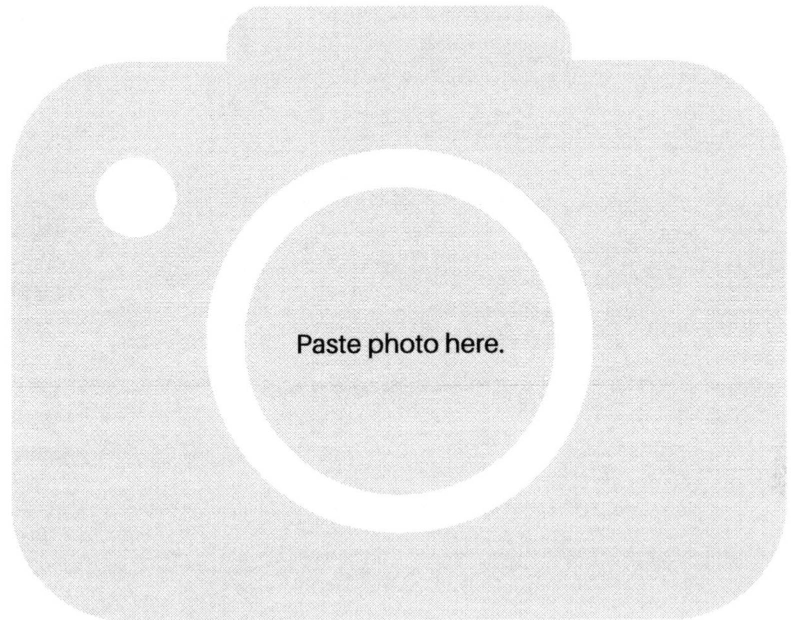
Paste photo here.

☆☆☆☆☆

Day 30

CANDLELIGHT

Candles give off a magical, warm and cosy light. Turn off or dim all other light sources. A little fuzziness in the candlelight isn't a bad thing, just make sure you have slow shutter speed and a still subject. And when you blow the candles out, there are more great moments to follow, just waiting to be captured in a photo.

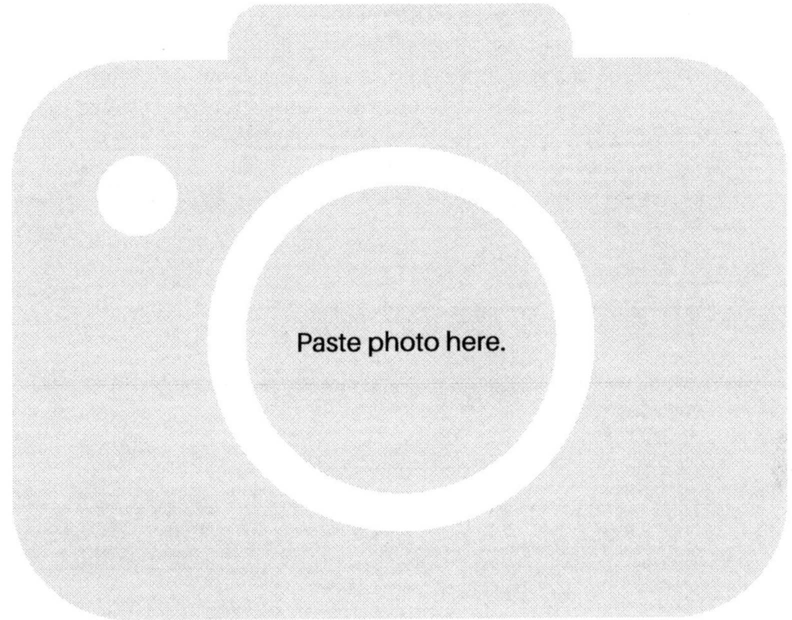
Paste photo here.

☆☆☆☆☆

Bonus Challenge 1

HOME SWEET HOME

What makes your home so special? Is it the complete package or individual elements? Is there something that, without it, it just wouldn't be the same? It is said that a house is a building but home is feeling. Capture that feeling of what home means to you.

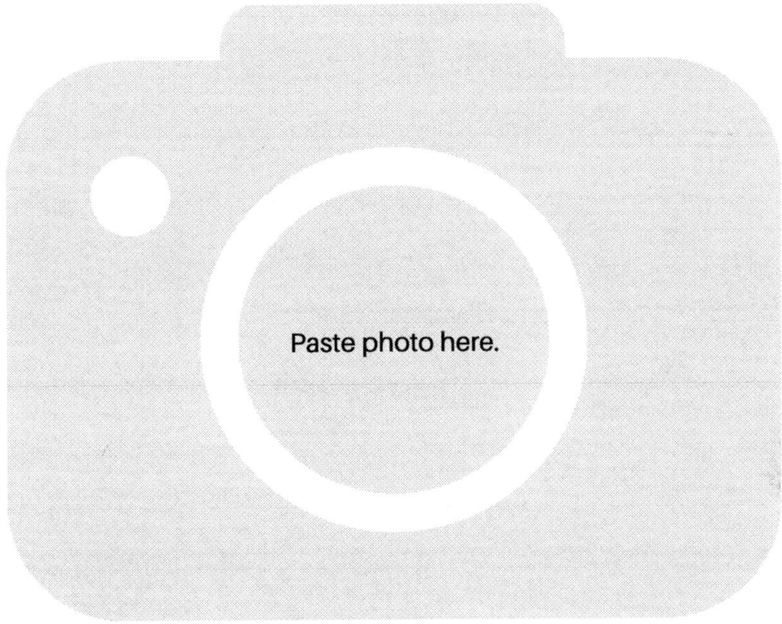
Paste photo here.

<u>Bonus Challenge 2</u>

OBJECTS IN THE AIR

A plane, a bird or a bee, in the magic of flight – each has its own settings to figure out. A hot-air balloon, fireworks and colorful kites also are unique to shoot. Soap bubbles floating in the air - come up with something to shoot, but also be confident enough to figure out how to shoot it well. In this challenge your eyes, and your skills, should be moving upwards...

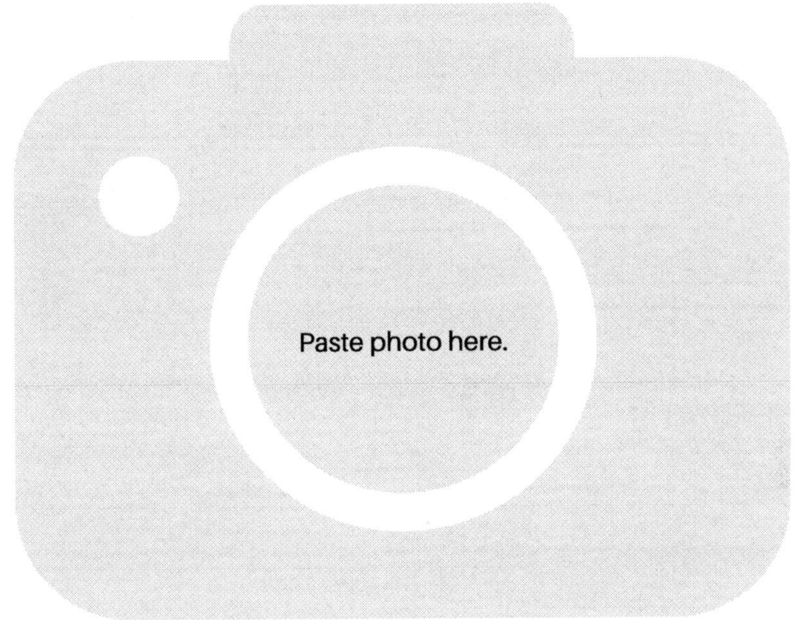
Paste photo here.

☆☆☆☆☆

Bonus Challenge 3

HIGH-ANGLE SHOT

A high-angle shot is when you are almost directly above your object. It changes everything, from the point of focus to the mood to the message you want to convey. It is easier to create dramatic effect and vulnerability from this angle. So pay close attention to the settings and effects you use and you will get the perfect shot!

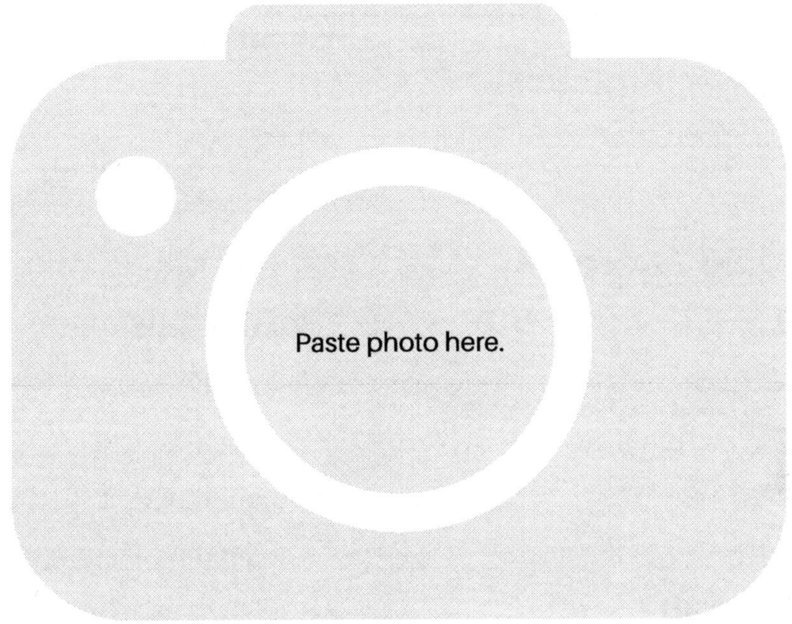
Paste photo here.

ASSIGNMENT OVERVIEW

1. Family
2. Clouds
3. Love
4. Black and White
5. Children
6. Green
7. Texture & Patterns
8. Babies
9. Landscape
10. Night Photography
11. Yellow
12. Seniors
13. Self-Portrait
14. Food Photography
15. Water
16. Street Photography
17. Architecture
18. Couples
19. Flash
20. Silhouette
21. Trees
22. Hands
23. Animals
24. Wind
25. Your Style
26. Spooky
27. Phone Photography
28. Beverages
29. Clothing
30. Candlelight

Home Sweet Home
Objects in the Air
High-Angle Shot

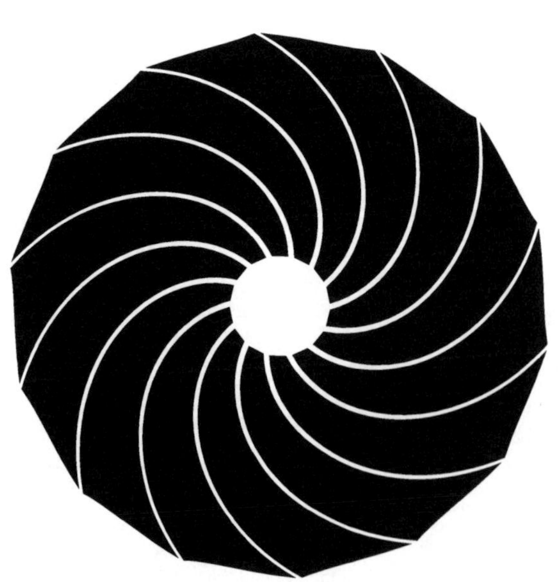

PHOTO IDEAS

BEST PHOTO LOCATIONS

FAVORITE QUOTES ABOUT PHOTOGRAPHY

NOTES

NOTES

NOTES

NOTES

We hope you enjoyed these assignments.
Your satisfaction is close to our hearts.

the odd
letter
co.

Don't forget to check out other books by
The Odd Letter Co. on Amazon!
If you have questions or comments
please send us an email at
sd.international.inc@gmail.com

Made in United States
Orlando, FL
05 December 2024